CYCLES OF THE SEASONS

by Golriz Golkar

The Child's World®
childsworld.com

Published by The Child's World®
1980 Lookout Drive • Mankato, MN 56003-1705
800-599-READ • www.childsworld.com

Photographs ©: Shutterstock Images, cover
(foreground), 1 (foreground), 14, 20 (Earth), 20
(Sun); Leonid Ikan/Shutterstock Images, cover
(background), 1 (background); iStockphoto,
5, 13; Max Shamota/Shutterstock Images,
6; Maryna Shkvyria/Shutterstock Images,
9; Andrij Vatsyk/Shutterstock Images, 10;
Kenneth Keifer/Shutterstock Images, 17;
Vladimir Melnik/Shutterstock Images, 18

ISBN 9781503828483
LCCN 2018944811

Printed in the United States of America
PAO2396

About the Author

Golriz Golkar is a teacher and children's
book author who lives in Nice, France. She
enjoys cooking, traveling, and looking for
ladybugs on nature walks.

Table of Contents

CHAPTER ONE

Why Seasons Occur

The planet Earth is always turning. Earth turns on its **axis** around itself and the sun. Earth is tilted at an angle that never changes. This tilt plays an important part in the different seasons.

When Earth turns around itself, it's called a **rotation**. It takes about 24 hours to complete. The side of the planet facing the sun experiences daytime. The side turned away from the sun experiences nighttime. At the same time, Earth moves around the sun. It takes 365 days for Earth to complete a **revolution** around the sun.

Earth's tilt toward and away from the sun makes the seasons change. Without this tilt, the seasons would be very different than they are. The areas near the polar regions would have winter all the time.

Summer occurs at different times of the year depending on where people live.

Without Earth's tilt, there would be too much heat and rain in the tropical **equator** region, disrupting the life cycle. Earth's tilt is important for balancing temperatures and helping nature survive.

At different times of the year, either the Northern or Southern **Hemisphere** is positioned closer to the sun based on Earth's tilt. The Northern Hemisphere is the upper half of Earth, from the equator to the North Pole. The Southern Hemisphere is the lower half of Earth, from the equator to the South Pole.

The United States is located in the Northern Hemisphere. When the Northern Hemisphere is closer to the sun, the United States experiences summer. As Earth continues turning around the sun, the Northern Hemisphere is no longer as close to the sun. But it's also not leaning away from it. This is when the fall season begins. A few months afterward, Earth will have turned so that the Northern Hemisphere is leaning away from the sun. At this time, winter begins. Finally, when this hemisphere is once again not positioned toward or away from the sun, spring arrives.

Some animals travel to different areas because of seasonal changes.

CHAPTER TWO

Seasonal Changes

Seasons may have different characteristics in different parts of the world. Some places may experience very hot summers. Other places may have extremely cold winters. However, there are certain patterns that occur during each season in most parts of the world.

In the Northern Hemisphere, winter begins in December. At this time, the hemisphere is positioned away from the sun. Temperatures are usually cold. It may rain and snow. There are fewer hours of daylight. Many animals **hibernate** during this time. Others go away to warmer places.

Bears are one animal that hibernates in the winter.

When Seasons Begin

The first day of winter and summer are each called a solstice. The winter solstice is the shortest day of the year, with the fewest hours of daylight. The summer solstice is the longest day, with the most hours of daylight. Spring and fall each begin on an **equinox**. On these days, the amounts of daylight and darkness are equal.

When spring arrives in March, plants grow and flowers bloom. The weather becomes warmer. Animals wake up or return from warmer locations. June brings the summer season. Since the hemisphere is positioned toward the sun, there are more hours of daylight. The temperatures may be the hottest of the year. In September, fall arrives. Temperatures cool. Animals prepare for cold weather by storing food. Winter is around the corner.

At any point in time, the season in the Northern Hemisphere is always the opposite of the season in the Southern Hemisphere. When it's summer in the United States, it's winter in Australia!

Many trees lose their leaves in the fall.

CHAPTER THREE
Different Seasonal Patterns

At the equator, temperatures remain about the same all year long. Locations near the equator have about the same amount of daylight and darkness all year. Since the equator is located around the middle of Earth, the planet's tilt remains at the same angle in this region all year long. The sun's rays do not have to travel far to reach the equator, so this direct sunlight makes the region warm year-round.

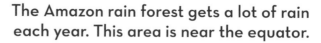
The Amazon rain forest gets a lot of rain each year. This area is near the equator.

Areas near the equator have rainy and dry seasons. During rainy seasons, an area will get more rain than at any other time of the year. During dry seasons there's not much rain. This can cause bodies of water, such as creeks, to dry up. Areas in Africa, Australia, Central America, and South Asia experience periods of heavy rainfall and dryness. This is caused by **monsoons**. These seasonal heavy winds are caused by changing temperatures over land and sea. They cause heavy rain in summer and dry spells in winter.

Seasons are also very different at the North and South Poles. At both poles, the summers are short and the winters are long. During the winter there is no sunlight at all. During the summer there are 24 hours of sunlight! But even when there is constant sunlight, the polar regions are always colder than most places on Earth because of the planet's tilt. Since the poles are located at the top and bottom on Earth, the sunlight is indirect. The sunlight is not as strong as it is at the equator, so the polar regions remain cold.

Summer monsoons can cause bad flooding.

CHAPTER FOUR

When Seasons Are Disturbed

It's important that seasons change as they are supposed to. Seasons are important to keeping life on Earth. Sometimes, unusual seasonal changes can harm nature. One example of a harmful, unusual seasonal change is when winters don't last as long as they should. Lakes that freeze in the winter are unfreezing earlier than they did in the 1980s. This change can kill cold-water fish.

Most scientists think unusual seasonal changes are caused in part by **climate change**. They believe that Earth's temperature is getting warmer as a result of human activities such as farming, burning trash, and driving cars. These activities cause dangerous gases to enter the air, creating unusual weather.

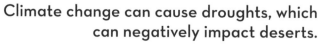
Climate change can cause droughts, which can negatively impact deserts.

In the United States, the shift from cold winter weather to warm spring weather is happening much sooner than it did decades ago. Glaciers and snow are melting in the polar regions. Oceans are becoming warmer. These changes make it difficult for some wildlife to survive. Normal cycles of the seasons are an important part of life on Earth. Without them, the life cycle would be out of balance.

Melting ice forces polar bears to swim longer distances.

Cycles of the Seasons

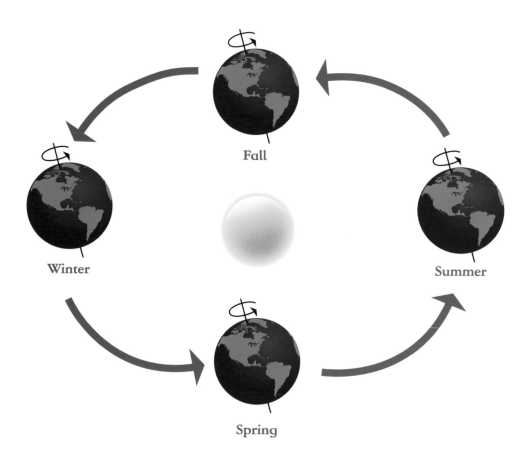

Earth's tilt causes different seasons. For example, the Northern Hemisphere will experience summer when Earth's axis is tilted toward the sun.

Fast Facts

- Earth is always turning on its axis at a tilted angle.

- As Earth revolves around the sun, changes in daylight, temperature, and weather cause seasons.

- Each season has unique patterns that repeat every year.

- The equator region is always warm.

- The polar regions are cold with extremes in daylight and darkness.

- Extreme heat or cold can harm nature and reduce food sources.

- Changes in the climate disturb the cycles of the seasons.

- Seasons are necessary for keeping life on Earth.

Glossary

axis (AK-sis) An axis is a real or imaginary line through the center of an object, around which the object turns. Earth makes a complete turn on its axis in about 24 hours.

climate change (KLY-mit CHAYNJ) Climate change is an increase in Earth's temperature resulting from human activities. Climate change can harm nature and decrease the supply of food for humans.

equator (i-KWAY-tur) The equator is the imaginary circle around Earth, halfway between the North and South Poles. Locations near the equator are warm because they get a lot of sunlight.

equinox (EE-kwuh-noks) The equinox is when the sun's rays hit the equator at an angle that makes both day and night 12 hours long. The first day of fall and spring are each called the equinox.

hemisphere (HEM-i-sfeer) A hemisphere is one-half of Earth. The United States is in the Northern Hemisphere.

hibernate (HYE-bur-nayt) To hibernate is to go through the winter in a resting state in order to save energy. During the winter, bears hibernate rather than hunt for food.

monsoons (mahn-SOONZ) Monsoons are wind systems over the Indian Ocean that bring both dry spells and heavy rains. Some parts of the world, such as South Asia, are affected by monsoons.

revolution (rev-uh-LOO-shun) Revolution is the movement of one object in outer space around another. Earth completes a revolution around the sun in one year.

rotation (row-TAY-shun) A rotation is one complete turn of Earth on its axis. Earth completes a rotation in about 24 hours.

To Learn More

IN THE LIBRARY

Furgang, Kathy. *Everything Weather*. Washington, DC: National Geographic, 2012.

Jemison, Mae. *Exploring Our Sun*. New York, NY: Children's Press, 2013.

Roker, Al. *Al Roker's Extreme Weather*. New York, NY: HarperCollins, 2017.

ON THE WEB

Visit our Web site for links about the cycles of the seasons:
childsworld.com/links

Note to Parents, Teachers, and Librarians: We routinely verify our Web links to make sure they are safe and active sites. So encourage your readers to check them out!

Index